# Makin Muffins

Written by Alison Hawes

You will need:

- milk
- fruit
- bowl
- cases
- spoons
- egg
- muffin mix

②

Wash your hands.

Put the oven on.

Put the cases in the tin.

Wash the fruit.

6

Put the muffin mix in the bowl.

Stir in the milk.

Put in the egg.

Stir in the fruit.

Put the mix in the cases.

Put the cases in the oven.

The muffins are cooked.

Put the muffins on the tray.

Wash the dishes.

⑮

Eat!

16